Made in the USA
Coppell, TX
07 October 2020

39193057R00111